Stitched and Beautiful

A journey of self-discovery and self-acceptance.

Micheline Montgomery
Kaja Montgomery *editor*

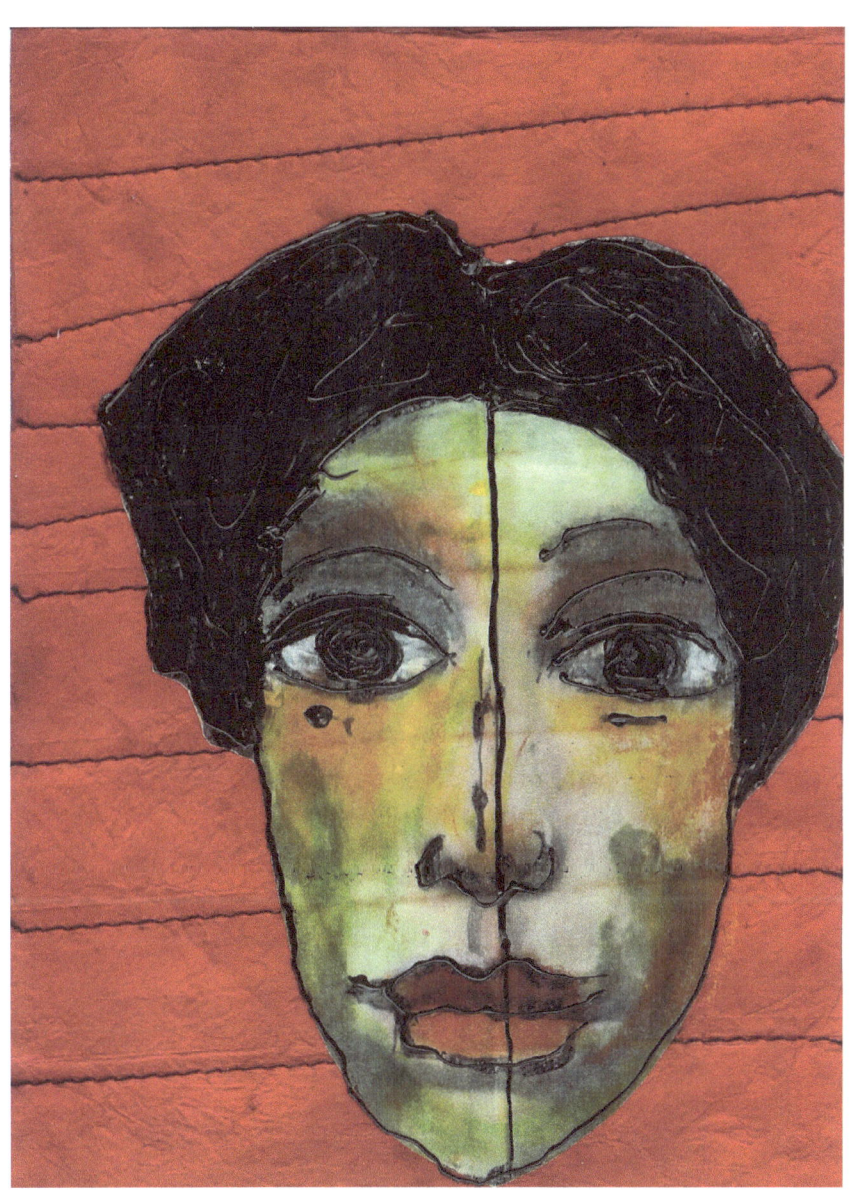

Table of Contents

Introduction

This artist book began one day when I came across the image of a woman's face for a make-up ad. It was artistically and boldly done and drew my attention. I cut out the image and reflected on it. For days I thought about women's aesthetic anxiety regarding the meaning of beauty. Are we that concerned about our outside look that we want to change the original mold?

Then I went to my journal: drawing, painting faces, cutting them up, gluing, tearing, photocopying, and taking sections. I used these pieces to create a new face, giving it a different personality. I played with all these ideas using some handmade paper I had been given.

As the book started to evolve, I began to call it Stitched and Beautiful. As we experience life we make attempts to better ourselves, inwardly, as well as outwardly through various means. Make-up, spa treatments, massage, yoga, travel to faraway places, spiritual retreats and even for some, plastic surgery.

There then comes a time when we have become stitched together. If we are fortunate enough, the stitches have blended. And the new face resembles the old one but filled with light and wisdom. This is how we can unfold into a transformed and peaceful self.

> A plastic flower might look pretty on first glance and will be around forever, but only a real flower which will wilt and drop its leaves soon after blossoming is truly beautiful.
>
> Lewis Richmond, Buddhist teacher

A Life of Passion

Passion for our endeavors comes from the fire inside our soul. It is expressed through our actions and shines through by being ourselves.

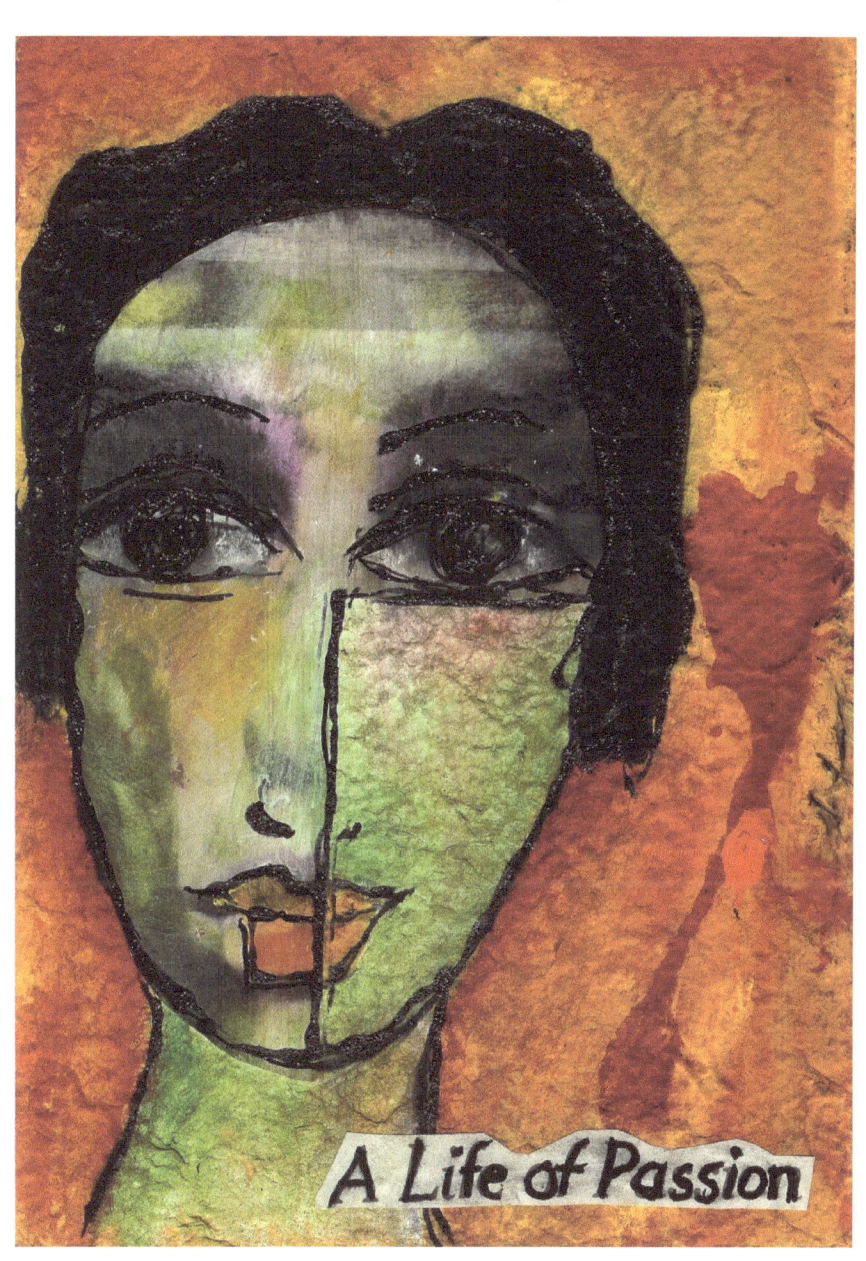

Sharing

Sharing with others, especially sharing ourselves, brings joy to the giver and the recipient. It helps create a sense of community and understanding of the different lives unfolding around us.

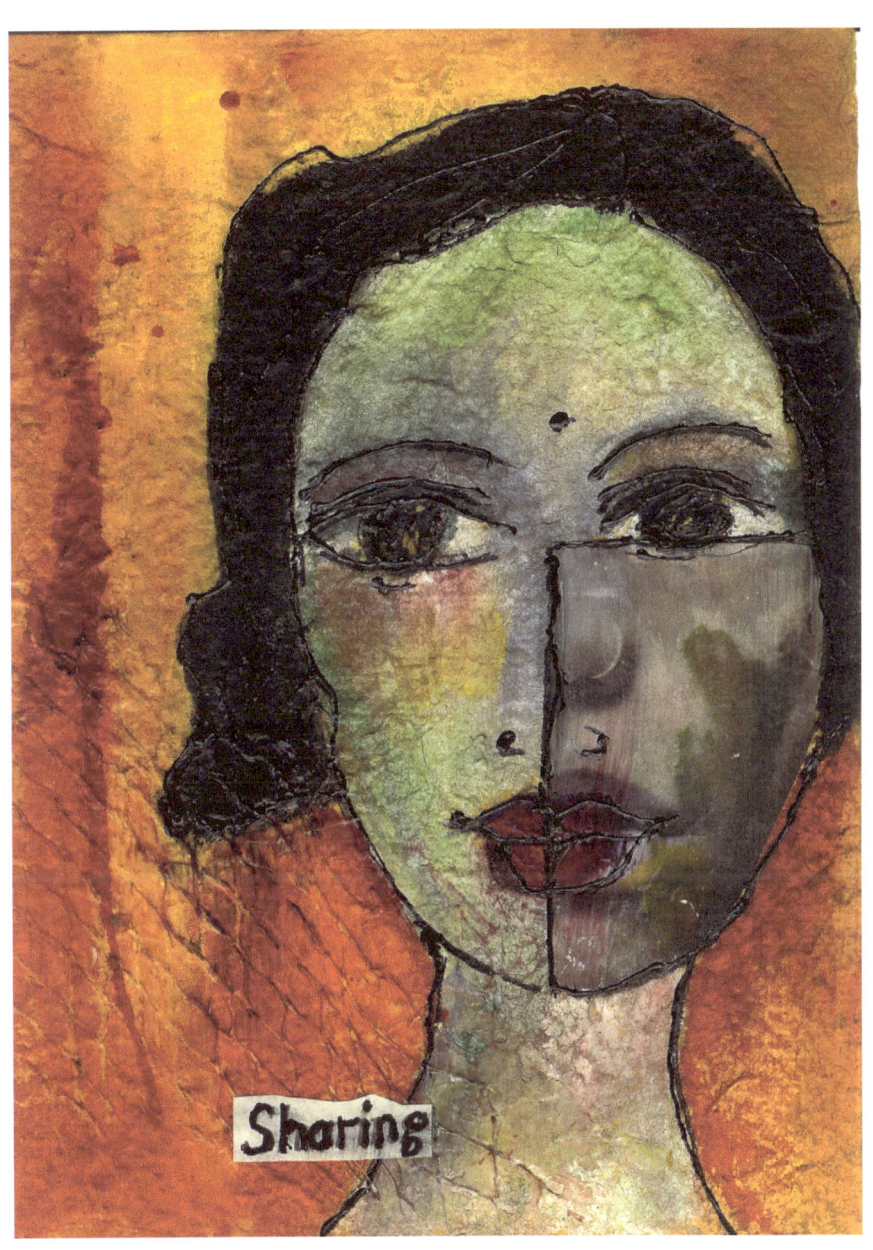

Fearless

When we trust the universe to send us its best, a strange thing happens, we become fearless and better able to face what may come.

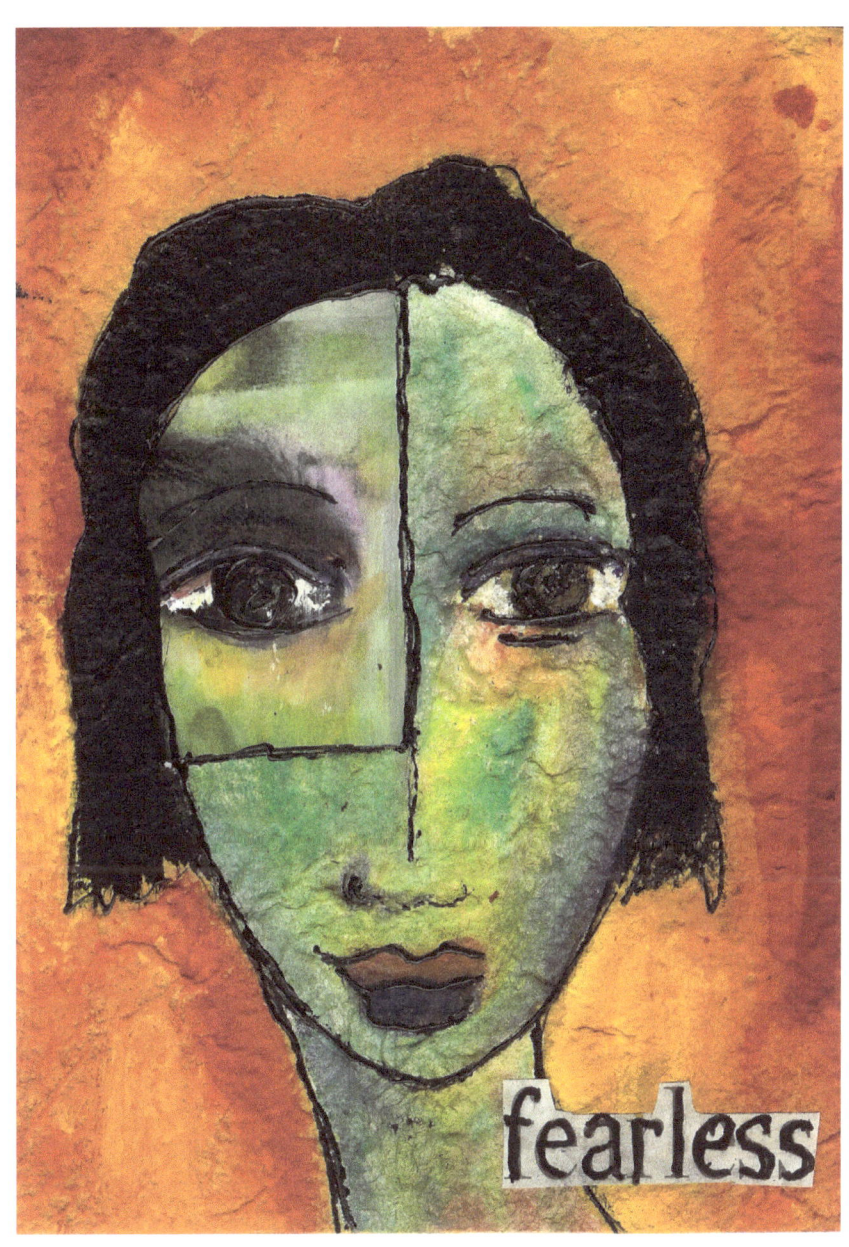

Cultural Pursuit

Be it travel, music, art, photography, acting, attending concerts, gallery events or other diverse community happenings, the pursuit of culture enriches our lives and deepens our understanding of humanity.

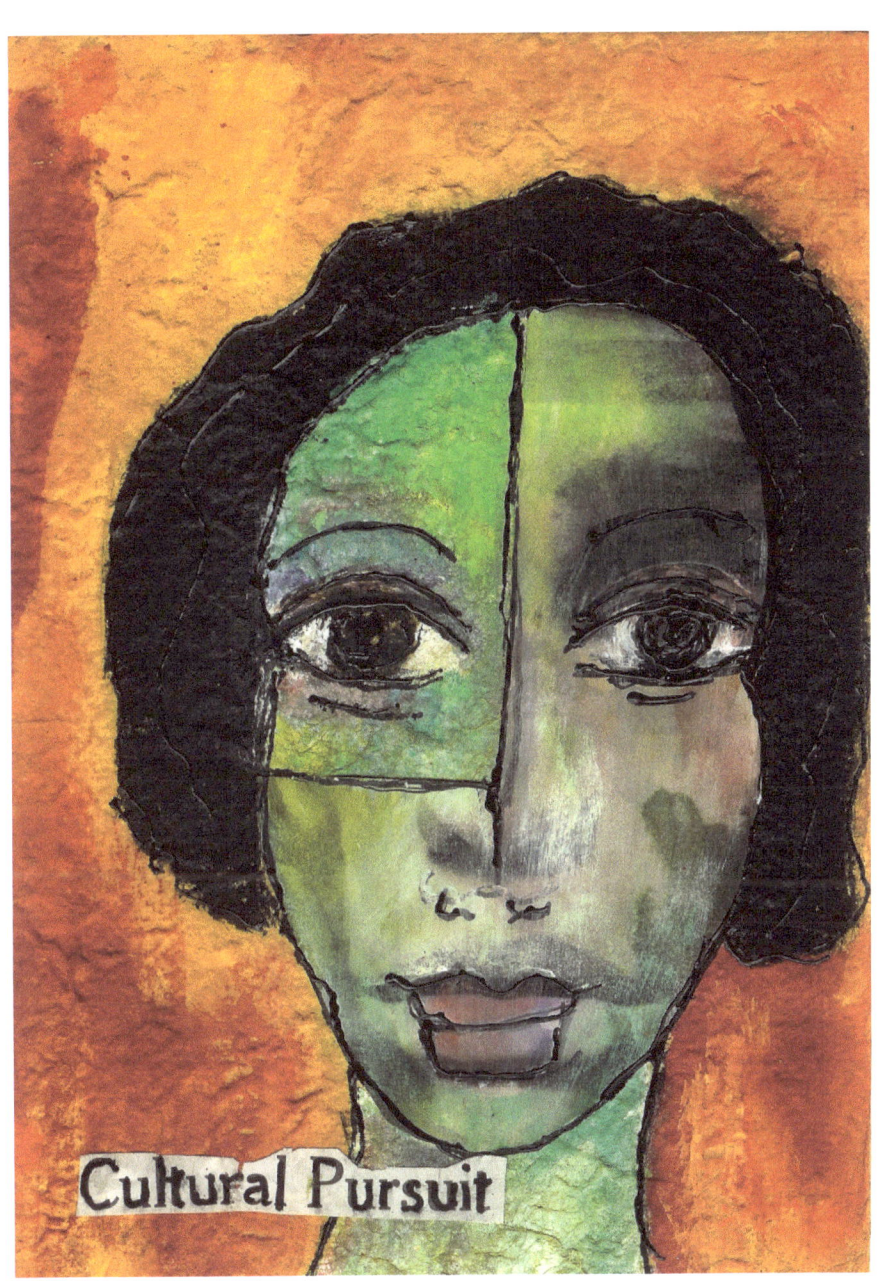

Cultural Pursuit

Laugh Out Loud

Laughter and humour are some of the healing tools we have to soothe our souls. They relax us and help to lessen frustrations while providing moments of delight.

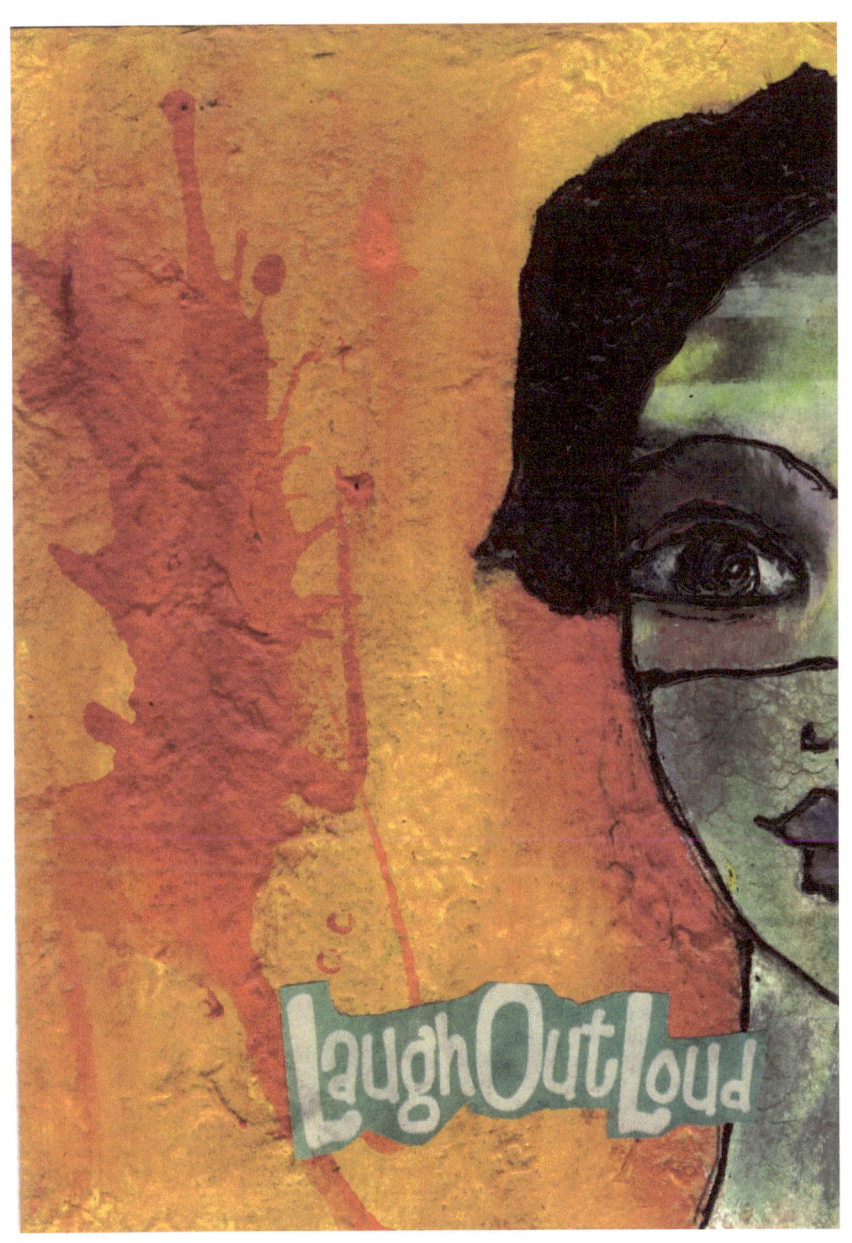

Joy Comes Out of the Blue

When we are open to life, beautiful and unexpected things happen. Like manna from heaven. Enjoy!

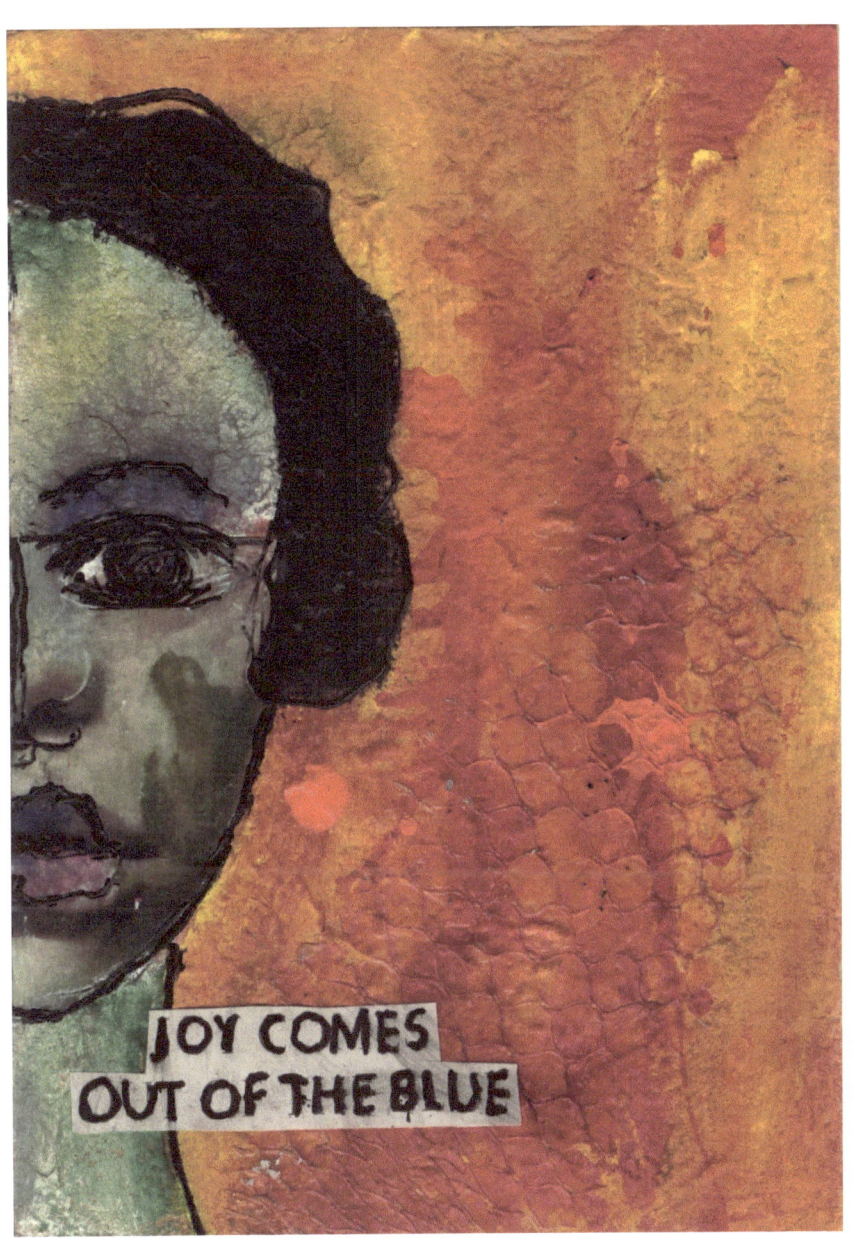

Natural Beauty

Beauty is an internal presence which radiates through to the outside.

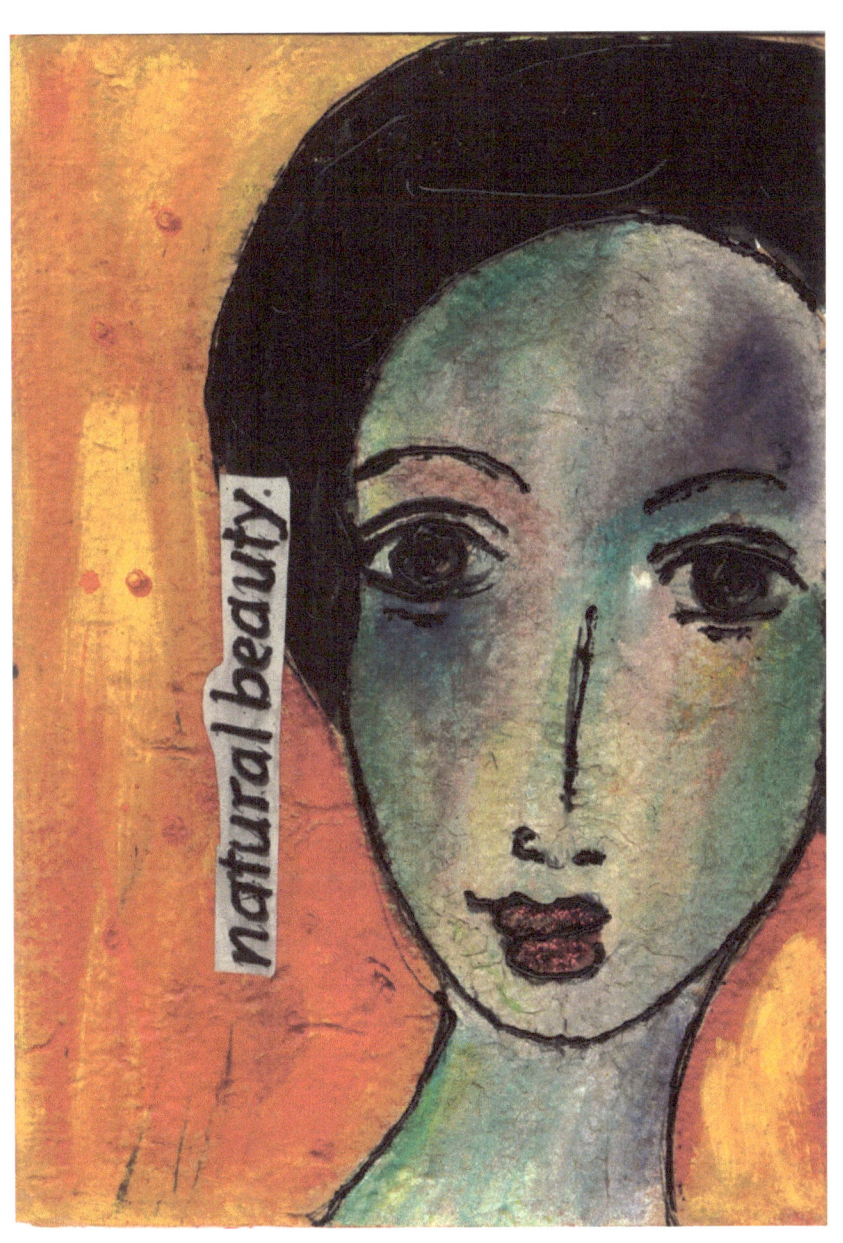

The Triumph of Good. Help People

We do not live in isolation. It is important to give of ourselves to others in any way we can and in as simple a way as we know. It will bring immense joy.

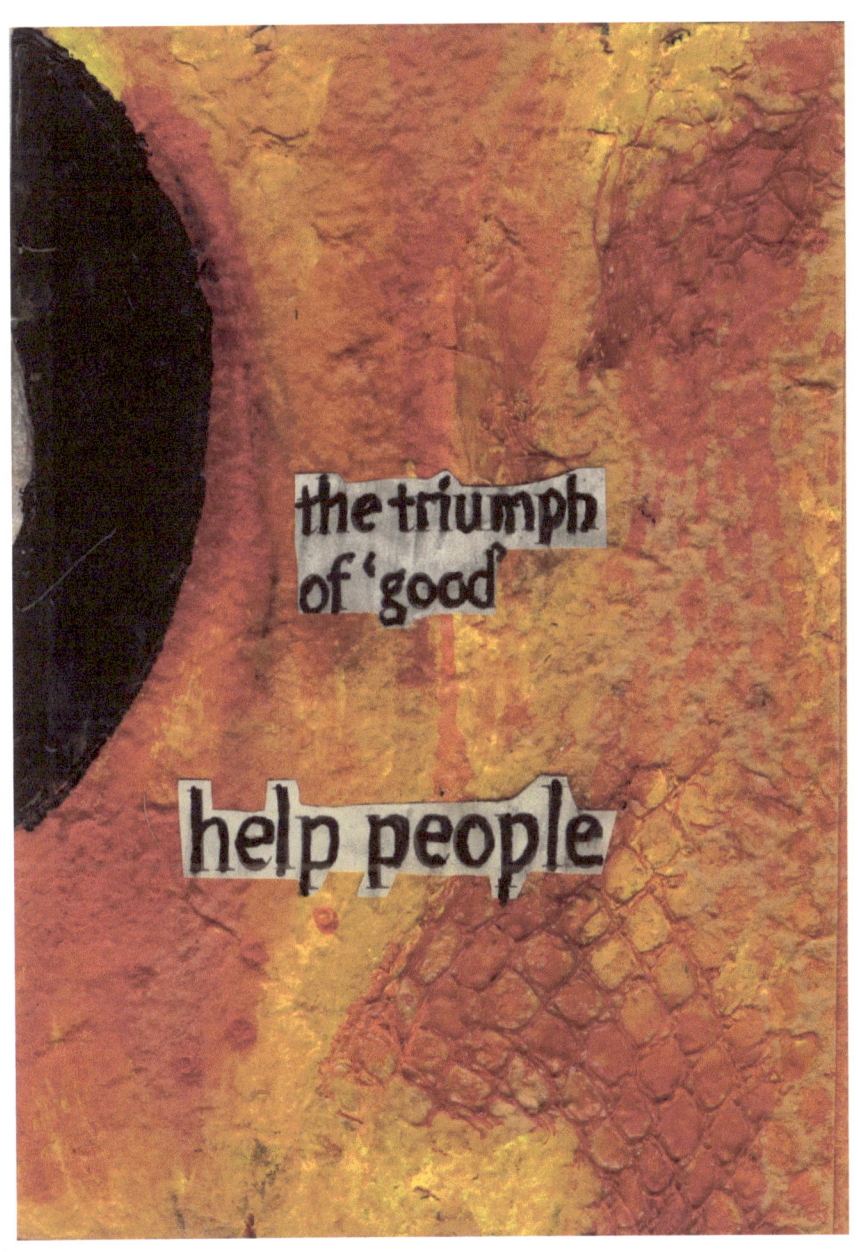

the triumph
of 'good'

help people

Balances

Equanimity between all things brings serenity.

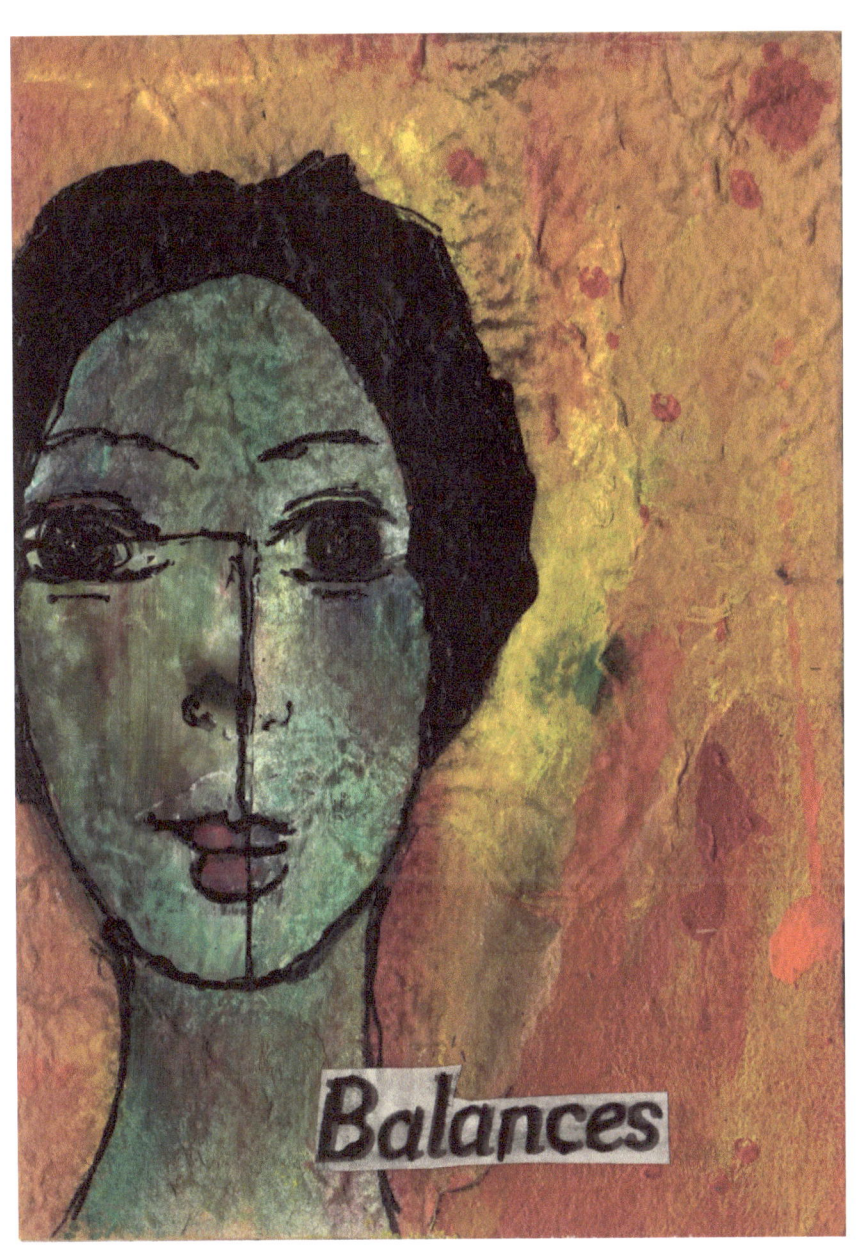

Journey

Life is a journey. In trusting the process, life becomes like a river flowing gently towards the ocean. Let life happen.

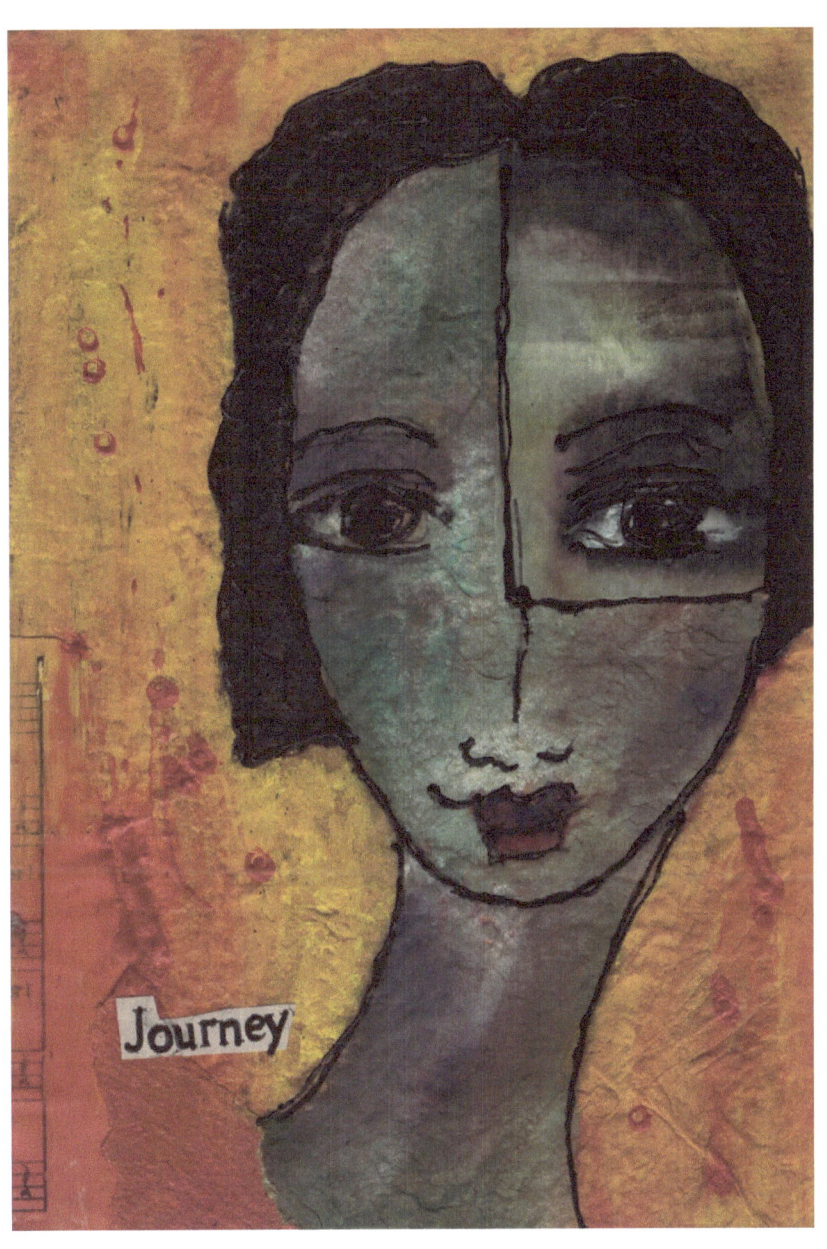

Peaceful Mystic. Visionary

A mystic is peaceful because of living unassumingly without having to prove anything to anyone. A mystic just IS.

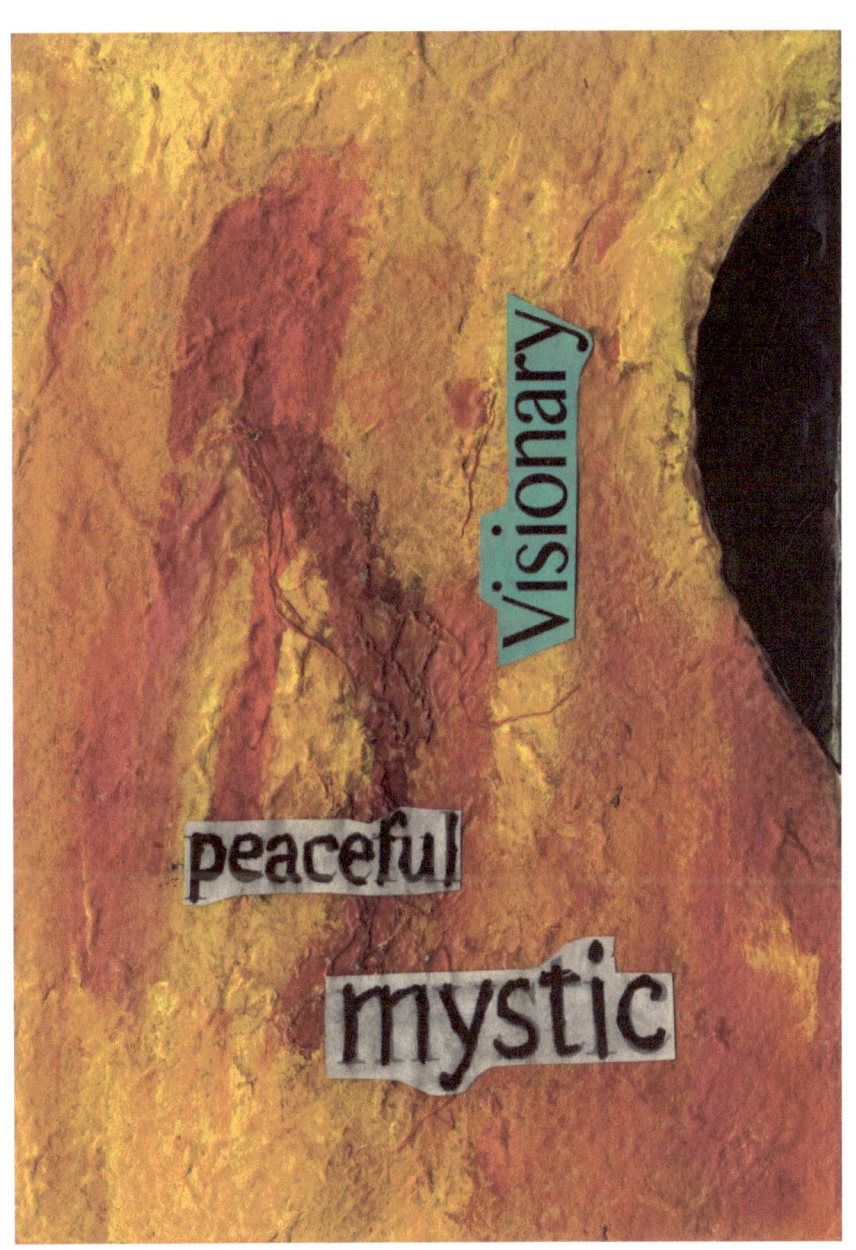

Be Yourself

Being ourselves should be our motto. Numerous temptations come our way to make us believe that external appearances matter more than the internal Self. Be wise and ignore them.

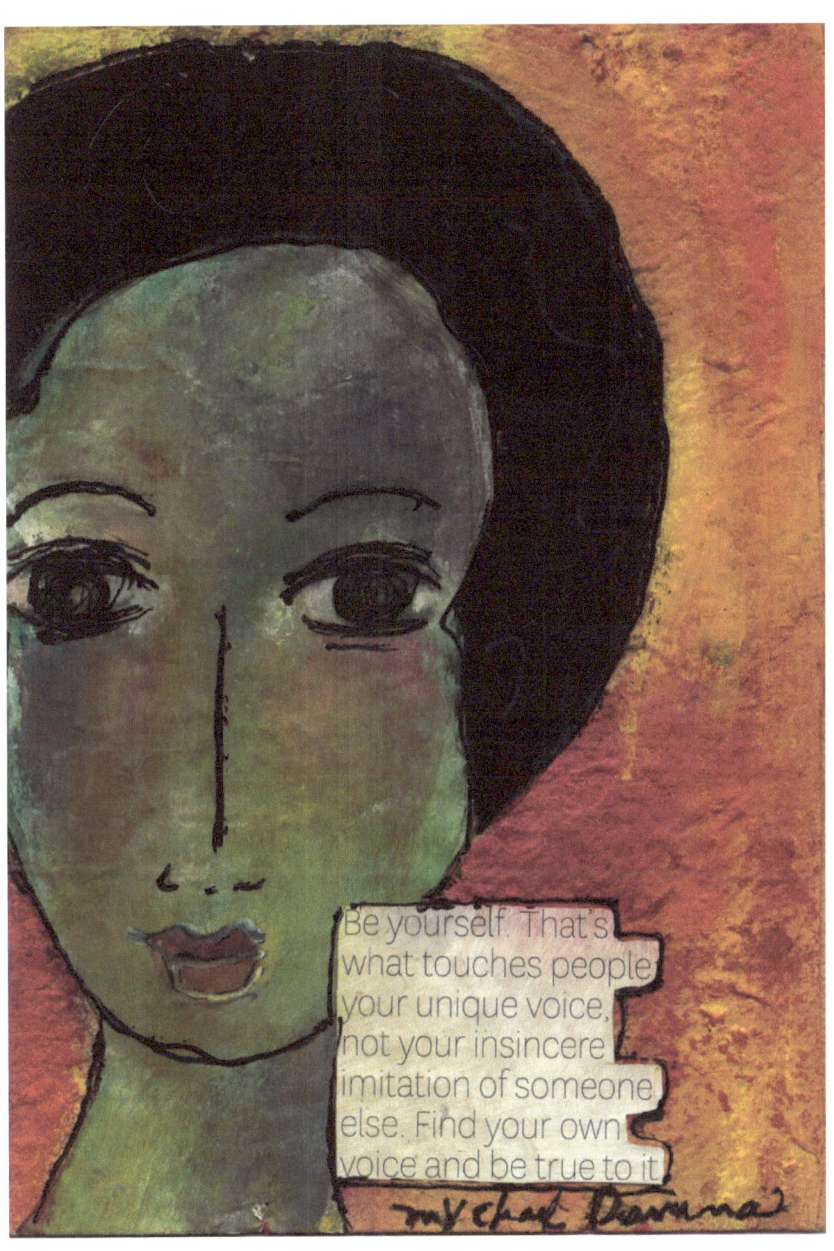

Be yourself. That's what touches people your unique voice, not your insincere imitation of someone else. Find your own voice and be true to it.

mychael Davina

Inspire

We inspire others by the way we live, passionately, simply, generously and with integrity. Sharing a smile with others is a bonus.

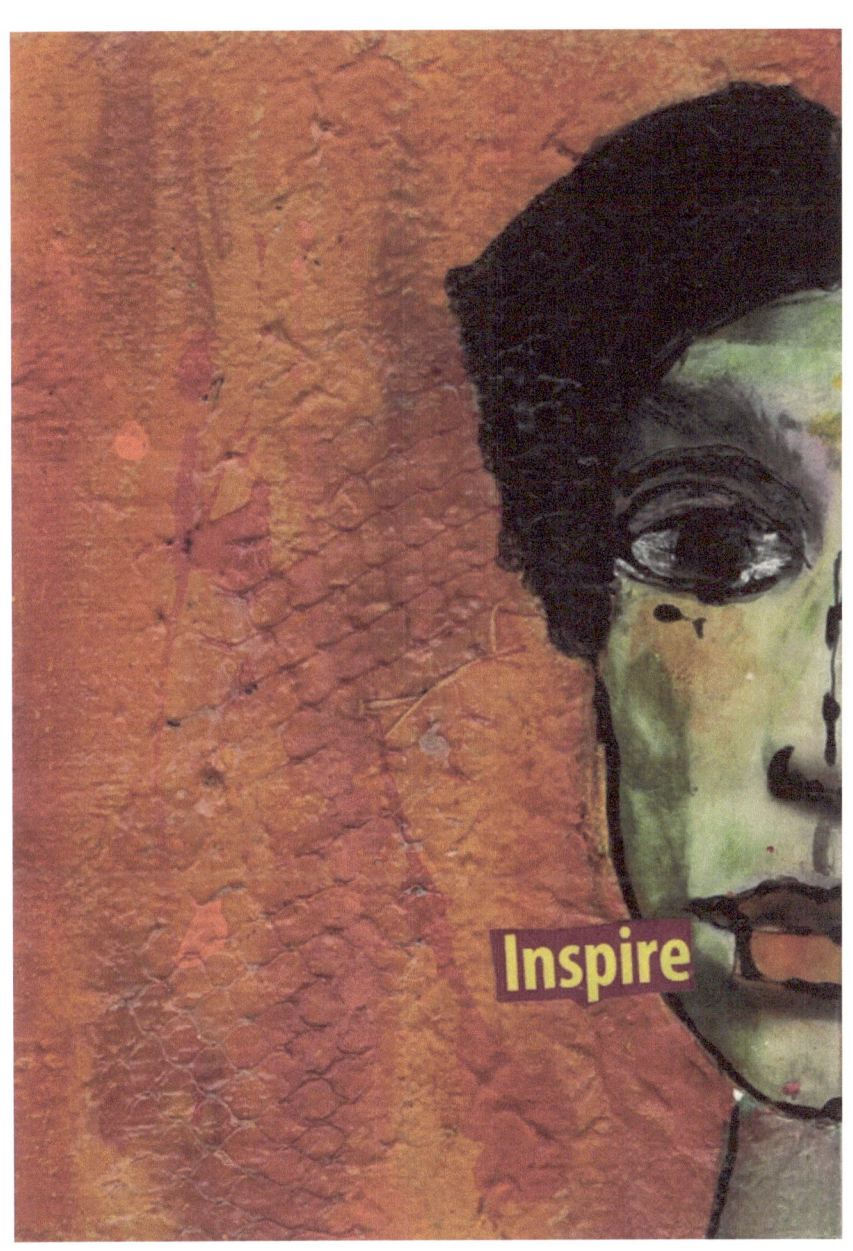

Creativity

A creative spirit not only comes through art, music and dance but shimmers through anything we enjoy doing be it cooking, teaching or problem solving.

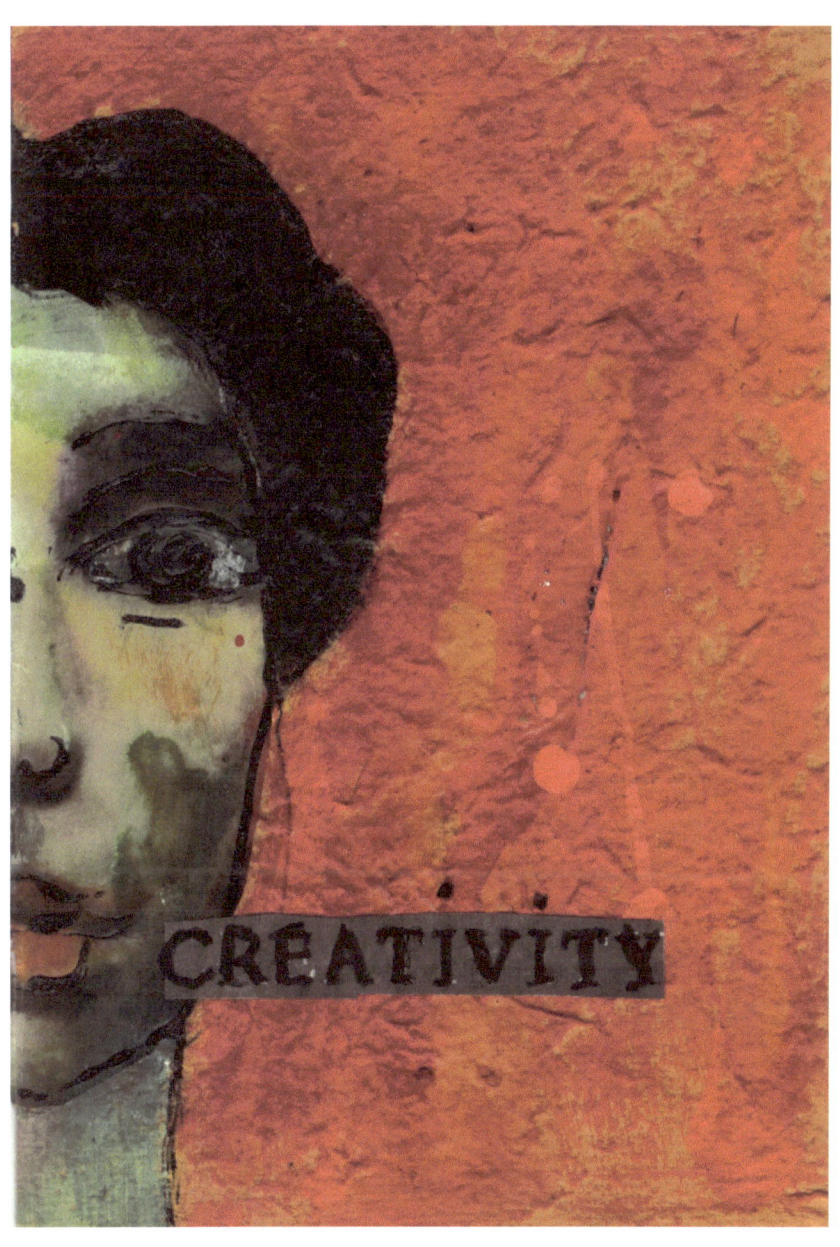

Soul Afire

A soul afire is a result of living life with integrity and passion. It has an amazing side effect of awakening joy in others.

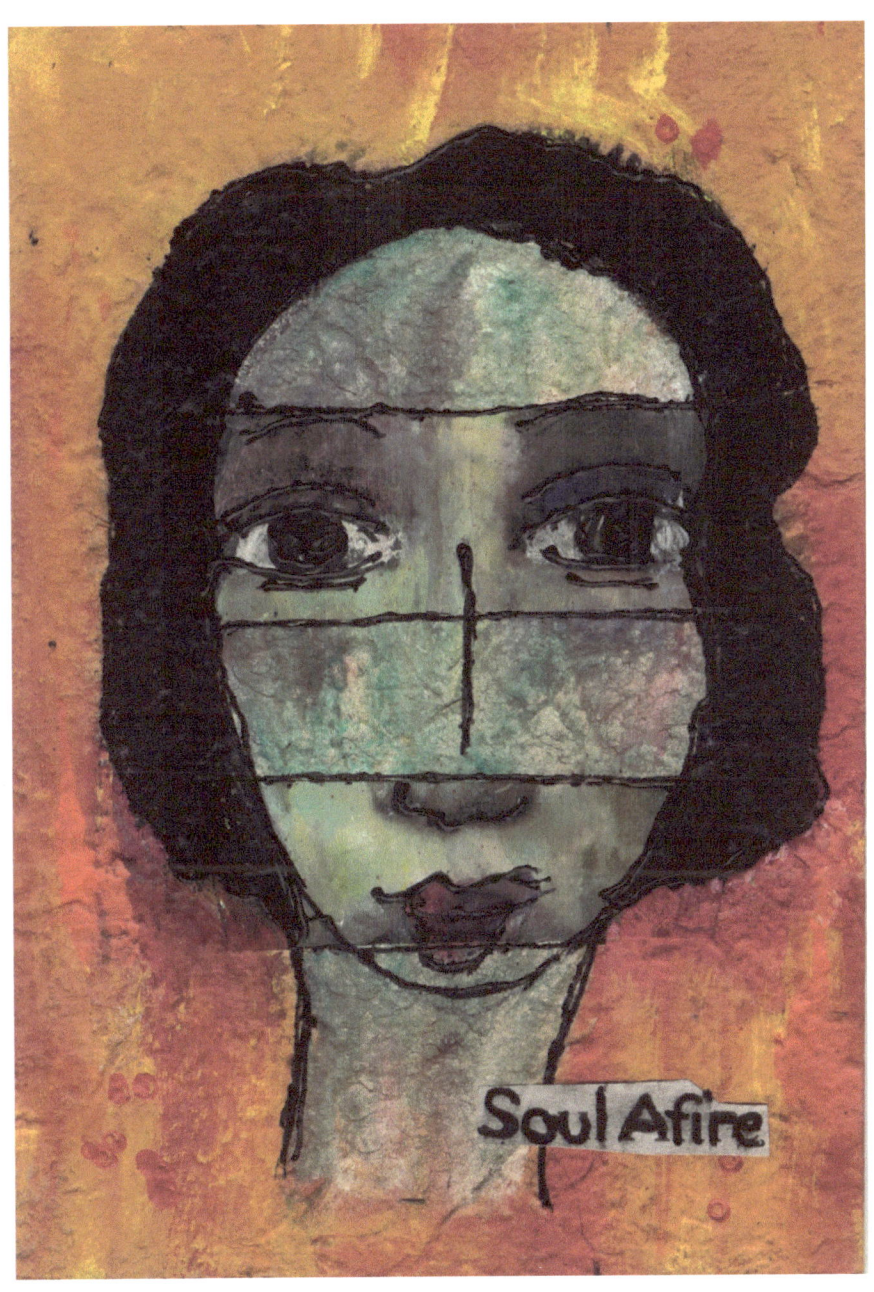

Soul Afire

Carry On

Indeed! By being fearless with a deep sense of self and others, carrying on almost becomes a breeze. Live life as if you are Michelangelo carving a block of marble. In the end you will have created a work of art. And it will be beautiful!

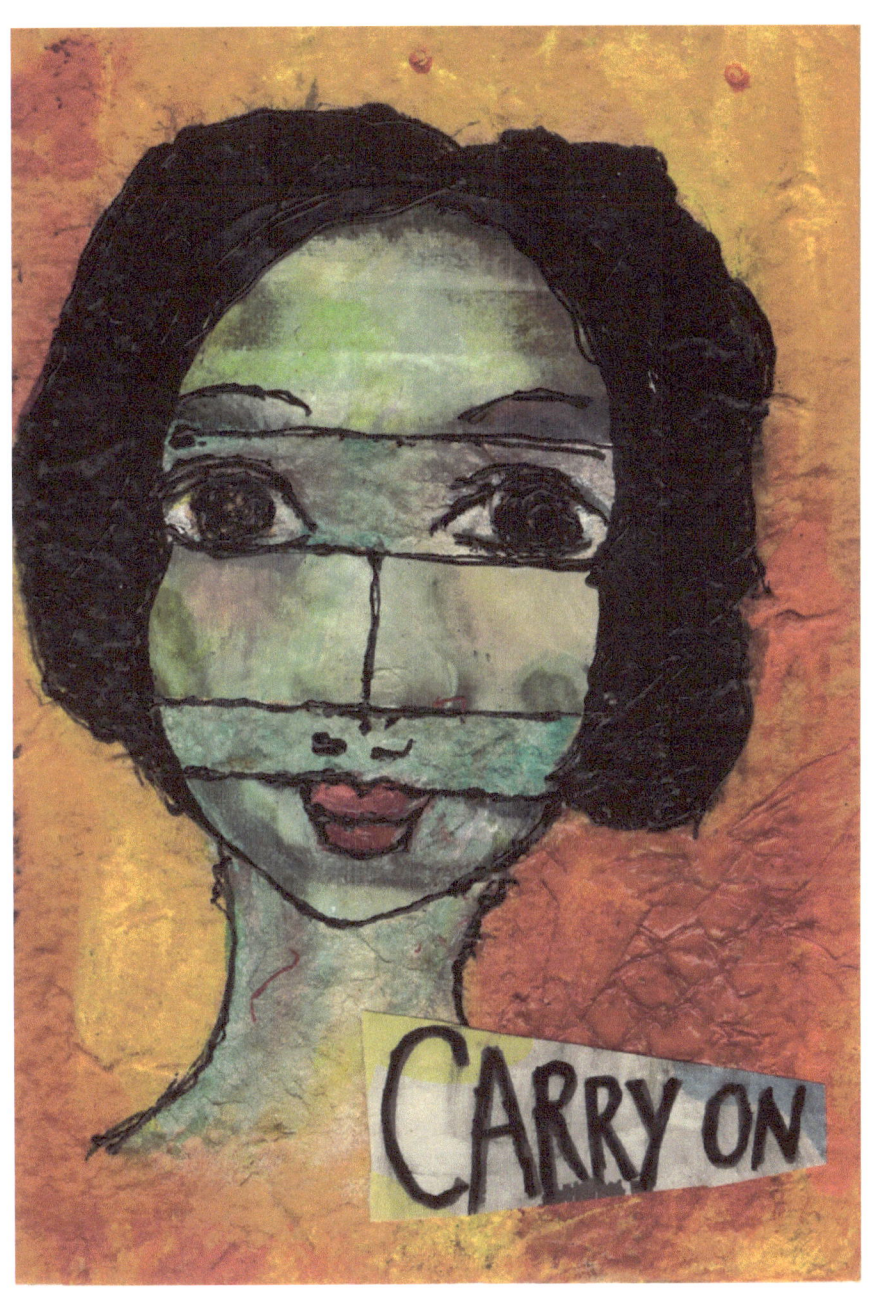

Micheline on Micheline

I have always created. I cannot separate art from life. I paint everywhere and on almost everything. I think of art when I wake up and dream of art when asleep. Buddhas, Angels, Nurses, Moms and Children are recurrent themes.

How I embrace life is how I express it through art. What interests me is how we transform the simple ordinary moments, as well as the complexities of life's journey into peaceful, beautiful and meaningful works of art. This endless spiritual quest remains an ever exciting and magical path.

As an artist, I make efforts to choose methods and materials that respect the earth. In my collage, I endeavor to use materials that are found, recycled and re-used, rather than bought. As well, I use water-based paints, acid free glue, cotton rag and stone paper. I am constantly seeking new ways to 'green' my art.

My life as an artist has been enriched by my long experience as a psychiatric nurse and my interest in human behaviour. I have a love of world travel and reading, especially biographies, art and spiritual books. I have been blessed with 3 children and 6 grandchildren who bring me immeasurable joy.

Kaja on Kaja

My mother and I have been collaborating since I was a child. She has always validated my ideas and helped them come to fruition. So it is with pleasure that I return the favour through designing and editing this book.

I am an artist in my mother's footsteps. My medium is sculpture. When an image surfaces in my mind, I let it guide my hands. As an art piece unfolds before me, it is one of the few times that I am truly living in the moment, completely focused on my task.

I am a full time teacher of kindergarten children with behavioural challenges. I enjoy helping these young souls become successful and start them on the journey of being the best that they can be.

I find peace in being in my backyard and creating a beautiful natural space filled with art. I am also a Flamenco dancer, have a passion for music and mother of 2 amazing boys.

Both Micheline's and Kaja's art can be viewed on their website.

www.pearangelartstudio.ca

Thank you to Stewart and Jojo for taking the time to read and comment. We appreciate your help.

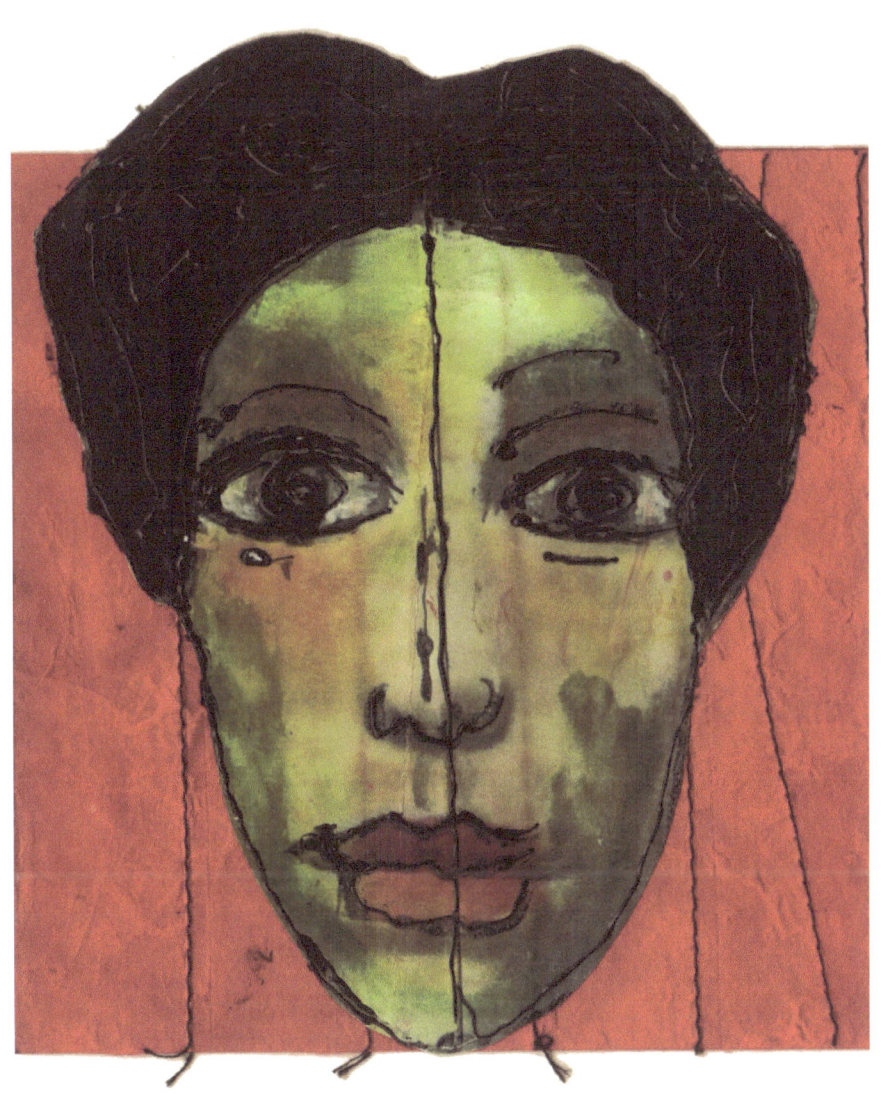

www.ingramcontent.com/pod-product-compliance
Lightning Source LLC
Chambersburg PA
CBHW040927180526
45159CB00002BA/645